# jQuery

## Tutorial for Beginners

Learn the Basics of jQuery and its Programming
Concepts in Simple and Easy Ways

# jQuery Tutorial

jQuery is a fast and concise JavaScript library created by John Resig' in 2006. jQuery simplifies HTML document traversing, event handling, animating, and Ajax interactions for Rapid Web Development.

# Audience

This tutorial is designed for software programmers who wants to learn the basics of jQuery and its programming concepts in simple and easy ways. This tutorial will give you enough understanding on components of jQuery with suitable examples.

# Prerequisites

Before proceeding with this tutorial, you should have a basic understanding of HTML, CSS, JavaScript, Document Object Model (DOM) and any text editor. As we are going to develop web based application using jQuery, it will be good if you have understanding on how internet and web based applications work.

# TABLE OF CONTENTS

# JQUERY - OVERVIEW

## WHAT IS JQUERY?

jQuery is a fast and concise JavaScript Library created by John Resig in 2006 with a nice motto: Write less, do more. jQuery simplifies HTML document traversing, event handling, animating, and Ajax interactions for rapid web development. jQuery is a JavaScript toolkit designed to simplify various tasks by writing less code. Here is the list of important core features supported by jQuery –

- DOM manipulation – The jQuery made it easy to select DOM elements, negotiate them and modifying their content by using cross-browser open source selector engine called Sizzle.
- Event handling – The jQuery offers an elegant way to capture a wide variety of events, such as a user clicking on a link, without the need to clutter the HTML code itself with event handlers.
- AJAX Support – The jQuery helps you a lot to develop a responsive and featurerich site using AJAX technology.
- Animations – The jQuery comes with plenty of built-in animation effects which you can use in your websites.
- Lightweight – The jQuery is very lightweight library - about 19KB in size (Minified and gzipped).
- Cross Browser Support – The jQuery has cross-browser support, and works well in IE 6.0+, FF 2.0+, Safari 3.0+, Chrome and Opera 9.0+
- Latest Technology – The jQuery supports CSS3 selectors and basic XPath syntax.

# How to use jQuery?

There are two ways to use jQuery.

- Local Installation – You can download jQuery library on your local machine and include it in your HTML code.
- CDN Based Version – You can include jQuery library into your HTML code directly from Content Delivery Network (CDN).

# Local Installation

- Go to the https://jquery.com/download/ to download the latest version available.
- Now put downloaded jquery-2.1.3.min.js file in a directory of your website, e.g. /jquery.

## Example

Now you can include *jquery* library in your HTML file as follows –

```
<html>
  <head>
    <title>The jQuery Example</title>
    <script type = "text/javascript" src = "/jquery/jquery-2.1.3.min.js">
    </script>

    <script type = "text/javascript">
      $(document).ready(function() {
        document.write("Hello, World!");
      });
    </script>
  </head>

  <body>
    <h1>Hello</h1>
  </body>
</html>
```

This will produce following result –

Hello, World!

2

# CDN BASED VERSION

You can include jQuery library into your HTML code directly from Content Delivery Network (CDN). Google and Microsoft provides content deliver for the latest version.

We are using Google CDN version of the library throughout this tutorial.

**Example**

Now let us rewrite above example using jQuery library from Google CDN.

```
<html>
  <head>
    <title>The jQuery Example</title>
    <script type = "text/javascript"
      src = "https://ajax.googleapis.com/ajax/libs/jquery/2.1.3/jquery.min.js">
    </script>

    <script type = "text/javascript">
      $(document).ready(function() {
        document.write("Hello, World!");
      });
    </script>
  </head>

  <body>
    <h1>Hello</h1>
  </body>
</html>
```

This will produce following result −

| Hello, World! |
| --- |

# HOW TO CALL A JQUERY LIBRARY FUNCTIONS?

As almost everything, we do when using jQuery reads or manipulates the document object model (DOM), we need to make sure that we start adding events etc. as soon as the DOM is ready.

If you want an event to work on your page, you should call it inside the $(document).ready() function. Everything inside it will load as soon as the DOM is loaded and before the page contents are loaded.

To do this, we register a ready event for the document as follows –

```
$(document).ready(function() {
   // do stuff when DOM is ready
});
```

To call upon any jQuery library function, use HTML script tags as shown below –

```html
<html>
  <head>
    <title>The jQuery Example</title>
    <script type = "text/javascript"
      src = "https://ajax.googleapis.com/ajax/libs/jquery/2.1.3/jquery.min.js">
    </script>
    <script type = "text/javascript" language = "javascript">
      $(document).ready(function() {
        $("div").click(function() {alert("Hello, world!");});
      });
    </script>
  </head>

  <body>
    <div id = "mydiv">
      Click on this to see a dialogue box.
    </div>
  </body>
</html>
```

This will produce following result when you click a dialogue box –

# HOW TO USE CUSTOM SCRIPTS?

It is better to write our custom code in the custom JavaScript file : custom.js, as follows –

```
/* Filename: custom.js */
$(document).ready(function() {
  $("div").click(function() {
    alert("Hello, world!");
  });
});
```

Now we can include custom.js file in our HTML file as follows –

```
<html>
  <head>
    <title>The jQuery Example</title>
    <script type = "text/javascript"
      src = "https://ajax.googleapis.com/ajax/libs/jquery/2.1.3/jquery.min.js">
    </script>

    <script type = "text/javascript" src = "/jquery/custom.js">
    </script>
  </head>

  <body>
    <div id = "mydiv">
      Click on this to see a dialogue box.
    </div>
  </body>
</html>
```

This will produce following result when you click a dialogue box –

## USING MULTIPLE LIBRARIES

You can use multiple libraries all together without conflicting each others. For example, you can use jQuery and MooTool javascript libraries together.

## WHAT IS NEXT ?

Do not worry too much if you did not understand above examples. You are going to grasp them very soon in subsequent chapters.

Next chapter would try to cover few basic concepts which are coming from conventional JavaScript.

# JQUERY - BASICS

jQuery is α framework built using JavaScript capabilities. So, you can use all the functions and other capabilities available in JavaScript. This chapter would explain most basic concepts but frequently used in jQuery.

## STRING

A string in JavaScript is an immutable object that contains none, one or many characters. Following are the valid examples of a JavaScript String –

```
"This is JavaScript String"
'This is JavaScript String'
'This is "really" a JavaScript String'
"This is 'really' a JavaScript String"
```

## NUMBERS

Numbers in JavaScript are double-precision 64-bit format IEEE 754 values. They are immutable, just as strings. Following are the valid examples of a JavaScript Numbers –

```
5350
120.27
0.26
```

## BOOLEAN

A boolean in JavaScript can be either true or false. If a number is zero, it defaults to false. If an empty string defaults to false. Following are the valid examples of a JavaScript Boolean –

```
true    // true
false   // false
0       // false
1       // true
""      // false
"hello" // true
```

# OBJECTS

JavaScript supports Object concept very well. You can create an object using the object literal as follows –

```
var emp = {
  name: "Zara",
  age: 10
};
```

You can write and read properties of an object using the dot notation as follows –

```
// Getting object properties
emp.name  // ==> Zara
emp.age   // ==> 10
```

```
// Setting object properties
emp.name = "Daisy"  // <== Daisy
emp.age  = 20     // <== 20
```

# ARRAYS

You can define arrays using the array literal as follows –

```
var x = [];
var y = [1, 2, 3, 4, 5];
```

An array has a length property that is useful for iteration –

```
var x = [1, 2, 3, 4, 5];

for (var i = 0; i < x.length; i++) {
  // Do something with x[i]
}
```

# FUNCTIONS

A function in JavaScript can be either named or anonymous. A named function can be defined using *function* keyword as follows –

```
function named(){
  // do some stuff here
}
```

An anonymous function can be defined in similar way as a normal function but it would not have any name.

A anonymous function can be assigned to a variable or passed to a method as shown below.

```
var handler = function (){
  // do some stuff here
}
```

JQuery makes a use of anonymous functions very frequently as follows –

```
$(document).ready(function(){
  // do some stuff here
});
```

# ARGUMENTS

JavaScript variable *arguments* is a kind of array which has *length* property. Following example explains it very well –

```
function func(x){
  console.log(typeof x, arguments.length);
}
func();          //==> "undefined", 0
func(1);         //==> "number", 1
func("1", "2", "3");  //==> "string", 3
```

The arguments object also has a *callee* property, which refers to the function you're inside of. For example –

```
function func() {
  return arguments.callee;
}

func();        // ==> func
```

# CONTEXT

JavaScript famous keyword this always refers to the current context. Within a function this context can change, depending on how the function is called –

```
$(document).ready(function() {
  // this refers to window.document
});
$("div").click(function() {
  // this refers to a div DOM element
});
```

You can specify the context for a function call using the function-built-in methods call() and apply() methods.

The difference between them is how they pass arguments. Call passes all arguments through as arguments to the function, while apply accepts an array as the arguments.

```
function scope() {
  console.log(this, arguments.length);
}
scope() // window, 0
scope.call("foobar", [1,2]); //==> "foobar", 1
scope.apply("foobar", [1,2]); //==> "foobar", 2
```

# Scope

The scope of a variable is the region of your program in which it is defined. JavaScript variable will have only two scopes.

- Global Variables – A global variable has global scope which means it is defined everywhere in your JavaScript code.
- Local Variables – A local variable will be visible only within a function where it is defined. Function parameters are always local to that function.

Within the body of a function, a local variable takes precedence over a global variable with the same name –

```
var myVar = "global";    // ==> Declare a global variable
function ( ) {
  var myVar = "local";   // ==> Declare a local variable
  document.write(myVar); // ==> local
}
```

## CALLBACK

A callback is a plain JavaScript function passed to some method as an argument or option. Some callbacks are just events, called to give the user a chance to react when a certain state is triggered.

jQuery's event system uses such callbacks everywhere for example –

```
$("body").click(function(event) {
  console.log("clicked: " + event.target);
});
```

Most callbacks provide arguments and a context. In the event-handler example, the callback is called with one argument, an Event.

Some callbacks are required to return something, others make that return value optional. To prevent a form submission, a submit event handler can return false as follows –

```
$("#myform").submit(function() {
  return false;
});
```

## CLOSURES

Closures are created whenever a variable that is defined outside the current scope is accessed from within some inner scope.

Following example shows how the variable counter is visible within the create, increment, and print functions, but not outside of them –

```
function create() {
  var counter = 0;

  return {
    increment: function() {
      counter++;
    },
        print: function() {
      console.log(counter);
    }
  }
}
var c = create();
c.increment();
c.print();   // ==> 1
```

This pattern allows you to create objects with methods that operate on data that isn't visible to the outside world. It should be noted that data hiding is the very basis of object-oriented programming.

## PROXY PATTERN

A proxy is an object that can be used to control access to another object. It implements the same interface as this other object and passes on any method invocations to it. This other object is often called the real subject.

A proxy can be instantiated in place of this real subject and allow it to be accessed remotely. We can saves jQuery's setArray method in a closure and overwrites it as follows –

```
(function() {
  // log all calls to setArray
  var proxied = jQuery.fn.setArray;
  jQuery.fn.setArray = function() {
    console.log(this, arguments);
    return proxied.apply(this, arguments);
  };
})();
```

The above wraps its code in a function to hide the *proxied* variable. The proxy then logs all calls to the method and delegates the call to the original method. Using *apply(this, arguments)* guarantees that the caller won't be able to notice the difference between the original and the proxied method.

## BUILT-IN FUNCTIONS

JavaScript comes along with a useful set of built-in functions. These methods can be used to manipulate Strings, Numbers and Dates.

Following are important JavaScript functions –

| Sr.No. | Method & Description |
|--------|---------------------|
| 1 | charAt()<br><br>Returns the character at the specified index. |
| 2 | concat()<br><br>Combines the text of two strings and returns a new string. |
| 3 | forEach()<br><br>Calls a function for each element in the array. |
| 4 | indexOf()<br><br>Returns the index within the calling String object of the first occurrence of the specified value, or -1 if not found. |
| 5 | length()<br><br>Returns the length of the string. |

| 6 | pop() |
|---|---|
| | Removes the last element from an array and returns that element. |
| 7 | push() |
| | Adds one or more elements to the end of an array and returns the new length of the array. |
| 8 | reverse() |
| | Reverses the order of the elements of an array -- the first becomes the last, and the last becomes the first. |
| 9 | sort() |
| | Sorts the elements of an array. |
| 10 | substr() |
| | Returns the characters in a string beginning at the specified location through the specified number of characters. |

| 11 | toLowerCase() |
|----|----|
| | Returns the calling string value converted to lower case. |
| 12 | toString() |
| | Returns the string representation of the number's value. |
| 13 | toUpperCase() |
| | Returns the calling string value converted to uppercase. |

# THE DOCUMENT OBJECT MODEL

The Document Object Model is a tree structure of various elements of HTML as follows –

```html
<html>
 <head>
   <title>The jQuery Example</title>
 </head>
 <body>
   <div>
    <p>This is a paragraph.</p>
    <p>This is second paragraph.</p>
    <p>This is third paragraph.</p>
   </div>
 </body>
</html>
```

This will produce following result –

---

This is a paragraph.

This is second paragraph.

This is third paragraph.

---

Following are the important points about the above tree structure –

- The <html> is the ancestor of all the other elements; in other words, all the other elements are descendants of <html>.
- The <head> and <body> elements are not only descendants, but children of <html>, as well.
- Likewise, in addition to being the ancestor of <head> and <body>, <html> is also their parent.
- The <p> elements are children (and descendants) of <div>, descendants of <body> and <html>, and siblings of each other <p> elements.

While learning jQuery concepts, it will be helpful to have understanding on DOM, if you are not aware of DOM then I would suggest to go through a simple tutorial on DOM Tutorial.

# JQUERY - SELECTORS

The jQuery library harnesses the power of Cascading Style Sheets (CSS) selectors to let us quickly and easily access elements or groups of elements in the Document Object Model (DOM).

A jQuery Selector is a function which makes use of expressions to find out matching elements from a DOM based on the given criteria. Simply you can say, selectors are used to select one or more HTML elements using jQuery. Once an element is selected then we can perform various operations on that selected element.

# The $() Factory Function

jQuery selectors start with the dollar sign and parentheses – $(). The factory function $() makes use of following three building blocks while selecting elements in a given document –

| Sr.No. | Selector & Description |
|--------|----------------------|
| 1 | **Tag Name** <br><br> Represents a tag name available in the DOM. For example $('p')selects all paragraphs <p> in the document. |
| 2 | **Tag ID** <br><br> Represents a tag available with the given ID in the DOM. For example $('#some-id') selects the single element in the document that has an ID of some-id. |
| 3 | **Tag Class** <br><br> Represents a tag available with the given class in the DOM. For example $('.some-class') selects all elements in the document that have a class of some-class. |

All the above items can be used either on their own or in combination with other selectors. All the jQuery selectors are based on the same principle except some tweaking.

**NOTE** – The factory function $() is a synonym of jQuery() function. So in case you are using any other JavaScript library where $ sign is conflicting with something else then you can replace $ sign by jQuery name and you can use function jQuery() instead of $().

## Example

Following is a simple example which makes use of Tag Selector. This would select all the elements with a tag name p.

```html
<html>
  <head>
    <title>The jQuery Example</title>
    <script type = "text/javascript"
      src = "https://ajax.googleapis.com/ajax/libs/jquery/2.1.3/jquery.min.js">
    </script>
    <script type = "text/javascript" language = "javascript">
      $(document).ready(function() {
        $("p").css("background-color", "yellow");
      });
    </script>
  </head>
  <body>
    <div>
      <p class = "myclass">This is a paragraph.</p>
      <p id = "myid">This is second paragraph.</p>
      <p>This is third paragraph.</p>
    </div>
  </body>
</html>
```

This will produce following result –

This is a paragraph.

This is second paragraph.

This is third paragraph.

# HOW TO USE SELECTORS?

The selectors are very useful and would be required at every step while using jQuery. They get the exact element that you want from your HTML document.

Following table lists down few basic selectors and explains them with examples.

| Sr.No. | Selector & Description |
|--------|------------------------|
| 1 | **Name** <br><br> Selects all elements which match with the given element Name. |
| 2 | **#ID** <br><br> Selects a single element which matches with the given ID. |
| 3 | **.Class** <br><br> Selects all elements which match with the given Class. |
| 4 | **Universal (*)** <br><br> Selects all elements available in a DOM. |
| 5 | **Multiple Elements E, F, G** <br><br> Selects the combined results of all the specified selectors E, F or G. |

# SELECTORS EXAMPLES

Similar to above syntax and examples, following examples would give you understanding on using different type of other useful selectors –

Here, you have different type of other useful selectors –
You can use all the above selectors with any HTML/XML element in generic way. For example if selector $("li:first") works for <li> element then $("p:first") would also work for <p> element.

# JQUERY - ATTRIBUTES

Some of the most basic components we can manipulate when it comes to DOM elements are the properties and attributes assigned to those elements.

Most of these attributes are available through JavaScript as DOM node properties. Some of the more common properties are –

- className
- tagName
- id
- href
- title
- rel
- src

Consider the following HTML markup for an image element –

```
<img id = "imageid" src = "image.gif" alt = "Image" class = "myclass"
 title = "This is an image"/>
```

In this element's markup, the tag name is img, and the markup for id, src, alt, class, and title represents the element's attributes, each of which consists of a name and a value.

jQuery gives us the means to easily manipulate an element's attributes and gives us access to the element so that we can also change its properties.

## GET ATTRIBUTE VALUE

The attr() method can be used to either fetch the value of an attribute from the first element in the matched set or set attribute values onto all matched elements.

## Example

Following is a simple example which fetches title attribute of <em> tag and set <div id = "divid"> value with the same value –

```html
<html>
  <head>
    <title>The jQuery Example</title>
    <script type = "text/javascript"
      src = "https://ajax.googleapis.com/ajax/libs/jquery/2.1.3/jquery.min.js">
    </script>

    <script type = "text/javascript" language = "javascript">
      $(document).ready(function() {
        var title = $("em").attr("title");
        $("#divid").text(title);
      });
    </script>
  </head>

  <body>
    <div>
      <em title = "Bold and Brave">This is first paragraph.</em>
      <p id = "myid">This is second paragraph.</p>
      <div id = "divid"></div>
    </div>
  </body>
</html>
```

This will produce following result –

| |
|---|
| *This is first paragraph.* |
| This is second paragraph. |
| Bold and Brave |

# SET ATTRIBUTE VALUE

The attr(name, value) method can be used to set the named attribute onto all elements in the wrapped set using the passed value.

## Example

Following is a simple example which set src attribute of an image tag to a correct location –

```
<html>
  <head>
    <title>The jQuery Example</title>
    <base href="https://www.mywebsite.com" />
    <script type = "text/javascript"
      src = "https://ajax.googleapis.com/ajax/libs/jquery/2.1.3/jquery.min.js">
    </script>

    <script type = "text/javascript" language = "javascript">
      $(document).ready(function() {
        $("#myimg").attr("src", "/jquery/images/jquery.jpg");
      });
    </script>
  </head>

  <body>
    <div>
      <img id = "myimg" src = "/images/jquery.jpg" alt = "Sample image" />
    </div>
  </body>
</html>
```

This will produce following result –

26

# APPLYING STYLES

The addClass( classes ) method can be used to apply defined style sheets onto all the matched elements. You can specify multiple classes separated by space.

**Example**

Following is a simple example which sets class attribute of a para <p> tag –

```
<html>
  <head>
    <title>The jQuery Example</title>
    <script type = "text/javascript"
      src = "https://ajax.googleapis.com/ajax/libs/jquery/2.1.3/jquery.min.js">
    </script>

    <script type = "text/javascript" language = "javascript">
      $(document).ready(function() {
        $("em").addClass("selected");
        $("#myid").addClass("highlight");
      });
    </script>

    <style>
      .selected { color:red; }
      .highlight { background:yellow; }
    </style>
  </head>

  <body>
    <em title = "Bold and Brave">This is first paragraph.</em>
    <p id = "myid">This is second paragraph.</p>
  </body>
</html>
```

This will produce following result –

| |
|---|
| *This is first paragraph.* |
| **This is second paragraph.** |

# ATTRIBUTE METHODS

Following table lists down few useful methods which you can use to manipulate attributes and properties –

| Sr.No. | Methods & Description |
|--------|------------------------|
| 1 | **attr( properties )**<br><br>Set a key/value object as properties to all matched elements. |
| 2 | **attr( key, fn )**<br><br>Set a single property to a computed value, on all matched elements. |
| 3 | **removeAttr( name )**<br><br>Remove an attribute from each of the matched elements. |
| 4 | **hasClass( class )**<br><br>Returns true if the specified class is present on at least one of the set of matched elements. |

| 5 | **removeClass( class )** Removes all or the specified class(es) from the set of matched elements. |
|---|---|
| 6 | **toggleClass( class )** Adds the specified class if it is not present, removes the specified class if it is present. |
| 7 | **html( )** Get the html contents (innerHTML) of the first matched element. |
| 8 | **html( val )** Set the html contents of every matched element. |
| 9 | **text( )** Get the combined text contents of all matched elements. |
| 10 | **text( val )** Set the text contents of all matched elements. |

| 11 | **val( )** |
|----|-----------|
|    | Get the input value of the first matched element. |
| 12 | **val( val )** |
|    | Set the value attribute of every matched element if it is called on <input> but if it is called on <select> with the passed <option> value then passed option would be selected, if it is called on check box or radio box then all the matching check box and radiobox would be checked. |

## Examples

Similar to above syntax and examples, following examples would give you understanding on using various attribute methods in different situation –

Here is a complete list of attribute methods in different situation –

| Sr.No. | Selector & Description |
|--------|------------------------|
| 1 | **$("#myID").attr("custom")**<br><br>This would return value of attribute *custom* for the first element matching with ID myID. |
| 2 | **$("img").attr("alt", "Sample Image")**<br><br>This sets the **alt** attribute of all the images to a new value "Sample Image". |
| 3 | **$("input").attr({ value: "", title: "Please enter a value" });**<br><br>Sets the value of all \<input\> elements to the empty string, as well as sets The jQuery Example to the string *Please enter a value*. |
| 4 | **$("a[href^=https://]").attr("target","_blank")**<br><br>Selects all links with an href attribute starting with *https://* and set its target attribute to *_blank*. |
| 5 | **$("a").removeAttr("target")**<br><br>This would remove *target* attribute of all the links. |
| 6 | **$("form").submit(function() {$(":submit",this).attr("disabled", "disabled");});**<br><br>This would modify the disabled attribute to the value "disabled" while clicking Submit button. |

| 7 | **$("p:last").hasClass("selected")** |
|---|---|
| | This return true if last <p> tag has associated class*selected*. |
| 8 | **$("p").text()** |
| | Returns string that contains the combined text contents of all matched <p> elements. |
| 9 | **$("p").text("<i>Hello World</i>")** |
| | This would set "<I>Hello World</I>" as text content of the matching <p> elements. |
| 10 | **$("p").html()** |
| | This returns the HTML content of the all matching paragraphs. |
| 11 | **$("div").html("Hello World")** |
| | This would set the HTML content of all matching <div> to *Hello World*. |
| 12 | **$("input:checkbox:checked").val()** |
| | Get the first value from a checked checkbox. |
| 13 | **$("input:radio[name=bar]:checked").val()** |
| | Get the first value from a set of radio buttons. |
| 14 | **$("button").val("Hello")** |
| | Sets the value attribute of every matched element <button>. |

| 15 | **$("input").val("on")** |
|----|---|
|    | This would check all the radio or check box button whose value is "on". |
| 16 | **$("select").val("Orange")** |
|    | This would select Orange option in a dropdown box with options Orange, Mango and Banana. |
| 17 | **$("select").val("Orange", "Mango")** |
|    | This would select Orange and Mango options in a dropdown box with options Orange, Mango and Banana. |

# JQUERY - DOM TRAVERSING

jQuery is α very powerful tool which provides α variety of DOM traversal methods to help us select elements in α document randomly αs well αs in sequential method. Most of the DOM Traversal Methods do not modify the jQuery object αnd they αre used to filter out elements from α document based on given conditions.

## FIND ELEMENTS BY INDEX

Consider α simple document with the following HTML content –

```
<html>
  <head>
    <title>The JQuery Example</title>
  </head>
  <body>
    <div>
      <ul>
        <li>list item 1</li>
        <li>list item 2</li>
        <li>list item 3</li>
        <li>list item 4</li>
        <li>list item 5</li>
        <li>list item 6</li>
      </ul>
    </div>
  </body>
</html>
```

This will produce following result –

- list item 1
- list item 2
- list item 3
- list item 4
- list item 5

- list item 6

---

- Above every list has its own index, and can be located directly by using eq(index) method as below example.
- Every child element starts its index from zero, thus, *list item 2* would be accessed by using $("li").eq(1) and so on.

## Example

Following is a simple example which adds the color to second list item.

```html
<html>
  <head>
    <title>The JQuery Example</title>
    <script type = "text/javascript"
      src = "https://ajax.googleapis.com/ajax/libs/jquery/2.1.3/jquery.min.js">
    </script>

    <script type = "text/javascript" language = "javascript">
      $(document).ready(function() {
        $("li").eq(2).addClass("selected");
      });
    </script>
    <style>
      .selected { color:red; }
    </style>
  </head>

  <body>
    <div>
      <ul>
        <li>list item 1</li>
        <li>list item 2</li>
        <li>list item 3</li>
        <li>list item 4</li>
        <li>list item 5</li>
        <li>list item 6</li>
      </ul>
    </div>
```

36

```
    </body>
    </html>
```

This will produce following result –

- list item 1
- list item 2
- list item 3
- list item 4
- list item 5
- list item 6

# FILTERING OUT ELEMENTS

The filter( selector ) method can be used to filter out all elements from the set of matched elements that do not match the specified selector(s). The *selector* can be written using any selector syntax.

## Example

Following is α simple example which αpplies color to the lists αssociated with middle clαss –

```html
<html>
  <head>
    <title>The JQuery Example</title>
    <script type = "text/javascript"
      src = "https://ajax.googleapis.com/ajax/libs/jquery/2.1.3/jquery.min.js">
    </script>

    <script type = "text/javascript" language = "javascript">
      $(document).ready(function() {
        $("li").filter(".middle").addClass("selected");
      });
    </script>

    <style>
      .selected { color:red; }
    </style>
  </head>

  <body>
    <div>
      <ul>
        <li class = "top">list item 1</li>
        <li class = "top">list item 2</li>
        <li class = "middle">list item 3</li>
        <li class = "middle">list item 4</li>
        <li class = "bottom">list item 5</li>
        <li class = "bottom">list item 6</li>
      </ul>
    </div>
  </body>
</html>
```

38

This will produce following result –

<div style="border:1px solid">

- list item 1
- list item 2
- list item 3
- list item 4
- list item 5
- list item 6

</div>

# LOCATING DESCENDANT ELEMENTS

The find( selector ) method can be used to locate all the descendant elements of a particular type of elements. The *selector* can be written using any selector syntax.

**Example**

Following is an example which selects all the <span> elements available inside different <p> elements –

```
<html>
  <head>
    <title>The JQuery Example</title>
    <script type = "text/javascript"
      src = "https://ajax.googleapis.com/ajax/libs/jquery/2.1.3/jquery.min.js">
    </script>
    <script type = "text/javascript" language = "javascript">
      $(document).ready(function() {
        $("p").find("span").addClass("selected");
      });
    </script>
    <style>
      .selected { color:red; }
    </style>
  </head>
  <body>
    <p>This is 1st paragraph and <span>THIS IS RED</span></p>
    <p>This is 2nd paragraph and <span>THIS IS ALSO RED</span></p>
```

```
    </body>
</html>
```

This will produce following result –

> This is 1st paragraph and THIS IS RED
>
> This is 2nd paragraph and THIS IS ALSO RED

# JQuery DOM Filter Methods

Following table lists down useful methods which you can use to filter out various elements from a list of DOM elements –

| Sr.No. | Method & Description |
|---|---|
| 1 | **eq( index )**<br><br>Reduce the set of matched elements to a single element. |
| 2 | **filter( selector )**<br><br>Removes all elements from the set of matched elements that do not match the specified selector(s). |
| 3 | **filter( fn )**<br><br>Removes all elements from the set of matched elements that do not match the specified function. |
| 4 | **is( selector )**<br><br>Checks the current selection against an expression and returns true, if at least one element of the selection fits the given selector. |

| 5 | **map( callback )**<br><br>Translate a set of elements in the jQuery object into another set of values in a jQuery array (which may, or may not contain elements). |
|---|---|
| 6 | **not( selector )**<br><br>Removes elements matching the specified selector from the set of matched elements. |
| 7 | **slice( start, [end] )**<br><br>Selects a subset of the matched elements. |

# JQUERY DOM TRAVERSING METHODS

Following table lists down other useful methods which you can use to locate various elements in a DOM –

| Sr.No. | Methods & Description |
|--------|----------------------|
| 1 | **add( selector )**<br><br>Adds more elements, matched by the given selector, to the set of matched elements. |
| 2 | **andSelf( )**<br><br>Add the previous selection to the current selection. |
| 3 | **children( [selector])**<br><br>Get a set of elements containing all of the unique immediate children of each of the matched set of elements. |
| 4 | **closest( selector )**<br><br>Get a set of elements containing the closest parent element that matches the specified selector, the starting element included. |

| 5 | contents( )<br><br>Find all the child nodes inside the matched elements (including text nodes), or the content document, if the element is an iframe. |
|---|---|
| 6 | end( )<br><br>Revert the most recent 'destructive' operation, changing the set of matched elements to its previous state. |
| 7 | find( selector )<br><br>Searches for descendant elements that match the specified selectors. |
| 8 | next( [selector] )<br><br>Get a set of elements containing the unique next siblings of each of the given set of elements. |
| 9 | nextAll( [selector] )<br><br>Find all sibling elements after the current element. |
| 10 | offsetParent( )<br><br>Returns a jQuery collection with the positioned parent of the first matched element. |

11    **parent( [selector] )**

Get the direct parent of an element. If called on a set of elements, parent returns a set of their unique direct parent elements.

12    **parents( [selector] )**

Get a set of elements containing the unique ancestors of the matched set of elements (except for the root element).

13    **prev( [selector] )**

Get a set of elements containing the unique previous siblings of each of the matched set of elements.

14    **prevAll( [selector] )**

Find all sibling elements in front of the current element.

15    **siblings( [selector] )**

Get a set of elements containing all of the unique siblings of each of the matched set of elements.

# JQUERY - CSS SELECTORS METHODS

The jQuery library supports nearly all of the selectors included in Cascading Style Sheet (CSS) specifications 1 through 3, as outlined on the World Wide Web Consortium's site.

Using JQuery library developers can enhance their websites without worrying about browsers and their versions as long as the browsers have JavaScript enabled.

Most of the JQuery CSS Methods do not modify the content of the jQuery object and they are used to apply CSS properties on DOM elements.

## APPLY CSS PROPERTIES

This is very simple to apply any CSS property using JQuery method css( PropertyName, PropertyValue ).

Here is the syntax for the method –

```
selector.css( PropertyName, PropertyValue );
```

Here you can pass *PropertyName* as a javascript string and based on its value, *PropertyValue* could be string or integer.

**Example**

Following is an example which adds font color to the second list item.

```html
<html>
  <head>
    <title>The jQuery Example</title>
    <script type = "text/javascript"
      src = "https://ajax.googleapis.com/ajax/libs/jquery/2.1.3/jquery.min.js">
    </script>

    <script type = "text/javascript" language = "javascript">
      $(document).ready(function() {
        $("li").eq(2).css("color", "red");
      });
    </script>
  </head>

  <body>
    <div>
      <ul>
        <li>list item 1</li>
        <li>list item 2</li>
        <li>list item 3</li>
        <li>list item 4</li>
        <li>list item 5</li>
        <li>list item 6</li>
      </ul>
    </div>
  </body>
</html>
```

This will produce following result –

| |
|---|
| • list item 1 |
| • list item 2 |
| • list item 3 |
| • list item 4 |
| • list item 5 |
| • list item 6 |

# APPLY MULTIPLE CSS PROPERTIES

You can apply multiple CSS properties using a single JQuery method **CSS( {key1:val1, key2:val2....)**. You can apply as many properties as you like in a single call.

Here is the syntax for the method –

**selector**.css( {key1:val1, key2:val2....keyN:valN})

Here you can pass key as property and val as its value as described above.

## Example

Following is an example which adds font color as well as background color to the second list item.

```html
<html>
  <head>
    <title>The jQuery Example</title>
    <script type = "text/javascript"
      src = "https://ajax.googleapis.com/ajax/libs/jquery/2.1.3/jquery.min.js">
    </script>
    <script type = "text/javascript" language = "javascript">
      $(document).ready(function() {
        $("li").eq(2).css({"color":"red", "background-color":"green"});
      });
    </script>
  </head>

  <body>
    <div>
      <ul>
        <li>list item 1</li>
        <li>list item 2</li>
        <li>list item 3</li>
        <li>list item 4</li>
        <li>list item 5</li>
        <li>list item 6</li>
```

```
      </ul>
    </div>
  </body>
</html>
```

This will produce following result –

| |
|---|
| • list item 1 |
| • list item 2 |
| list item |
| • list item 4 |
| • list item 5 |
| • list item 6 |

# SETTING ELEMENT WIDTH & HEIGHT

The **width( val )** and **height( val )** method can be used to set the width and height respectively of any element.

## Example

Following is a simple example which sets the width of first division element where as rest of the elements have width set by style sheet

```
<html>
  <head>
    <title>The jQuery Example</title>
    <script type = "text/javascript"
      src = "https://ajax.googleapis.com/ajax/libs/jquery/2.1.3/jquery.min.js">
    </script>

    <script type = "text/javascript" language = "javascript">
      $(document).ready(function() {
        $("div:first").width(100);
        $("div:first").css("background-color", "blue");
      });
    </script>

    <style>
      div {
        width:70px; height:50px; float:left;
        margin:5px; background:red; cursor:pointer;
      }
    </style>
  </head>

  <body>
    <div></div>
    <div>d</div>
    <div>d</div>
    <div>d</div>
    <div>d</div>
  </body>
</html>
```

This will produce following result –

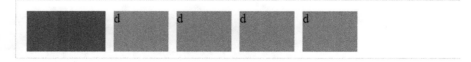

# JQUERY CSS METHODS

Following table lists down all the methods which you can use to play with CSS properties –

| Sr.No. | Method & Description |
|--------|---------------------|
| 1 | **css( name )** <br><br> Return a style property on the first matched element. |
| 2 | **css( name, value )** <br><br> Set a single style property to a value on all matched elements. |
| 3 | **css( properties )** <br><br> Set a key/value object as style properties to all matched elements. |
| 4 | **height( val )** <br><br> Set the CSS height of every matched element. |

| 5 | **height( )** |
|---|---|
| | Get the current computed, pixel, height of the first matched element. |

| 6 | **innerHeight( )** |
|---|---|
| | Gets the inner height (excludes the border and includes the padding) for the first matched element. |

| 7 | **innerWidth( )** |
|---|---|
| | Gets the inner width (excludes the border and includes the padding) for the first matched element. |

| 8 | **offset( )** |
|---|---|
| | Get the current offset of the first matched element, in pixels, relative to the document. |

| 9 | **offsetParent( )** |
|---|---|
| | Returns a jQuery collection with the positioned parent of the first matched element. |

| 10 | **outerHeight( [margin] )**<br><br>Gets the outer height (includes the border and padding by default) for the first matched element. |
|---|---|
| 11 | **outerWidth( [margin] )**<br><br>Get the outer width (includes the border and padding by default) for the first matched element. |
| 12 | **position( )**<br><br>Gets the top and left position of an element relative to its offset parent. |
| 13 | **scrollLeft( val )**<br><br>When a value is passed in, the scroll left offset is set to that value on all matched elements. |
| 14 | **scrollLeft( )**<br><br>Gets the scroll left offset of the first matched element. |
| 15 | **scrollTop( val )**<br><br>When a value is passed in, the scroll top offset is set to that value on all matched elements. |

| 16 | **scrollTop( )** |
|---|---|
| | Gets the scroll top offset of the first matched element. |
| 17 | **width( val )** |
| | Set the CSS width of every matched element. |
| 18 | **width( )** |
| | Get the current computed, pixel, width of the first matched element. |

# JQUERY - DOM MANIPULATION

JQuery provides methods to manipulate DOM in efficient way. You do not need to write big code to modify the value of any element's attribute or to extract HTML code from a paragraph or division.

JQuery provides methods such as .attr(), .html(), and .val() which act as getters, retrieving information from DOM elements for later use.

## CONTENT MANIPULATION

The html( ) method gets the html contents (innerHTML) of the first matched element.

Here is the syntax for the method –

   *selector*.html( )

### Example

Following is an example which makes use of .html() and .text(val) methods. Here .html() retrieves HTML content from the object and then .text( val ) method sets value of the object using passed parameter –

```
<html>
  <head>
    <title>The jQuery Example</title>
    <script type = "text/javascript"
     src =
"https://ajax.googleapis.com/ajax/libs/jquery/2.1.3/jquery.min.js">
    </script>

    <script type = "text/javascript" language = "javascript">
      $(document).ready(function() {
        $("div").click(function () {
          var content = $(this).html();
          $("#result").text( content );
```

```
        });
      });
    </script>

    <style>
      #division{ margin:10px;padding:12px; border:2px solid #666;
width:60px;}
    </style>
  </head>

  <body>
    <p>Click on the square below:</p>
    <span id = "result"> </span>

    <div id = "division" style = "background-color:blue;">
      This is Blue Square!!
    </div>
  </body>
</html>
```

This will produce following result –

Click on the square below –

This is Blue Square!!

Result after clickiing the square:

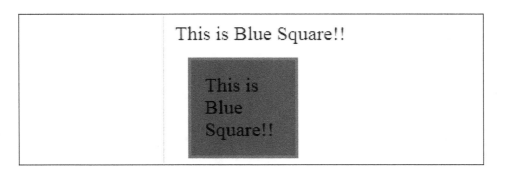

# DOM ELEMENT REPLACEMENT

You can replace a complete DOM element with the specified HTML or DOM elements. The replaceWith( content ) method serves this purpose very well.

Here is the syntax for the method –

*selector*.replaceWith( content )

Here content is what you want to have instead of original element. This could be HTML or simple text.

**Example**

Following is an example which would replace division element with "<h1>JQuery is Great </h1>" –

```
<html>
  <head>
    <title>The jQuery Example</title>
    <script type = "text/javascript"
      src = "https://ajax.googleapis.com/ajax/libs/jquery/2.1.3/jquery.min.js">
    </script>

    <script type = "text/javascript" language = "javascript">
      $(document).ready(function() {
        $("div").click(function () {
          $(this).replaceWith("<h1>JQuery is Great</h1>");
        });
      });
```

```
    </script>
    <style>
      #division{ margin:10px;padding:12px; border:2px solid #666;
width:60px;}
    </style>
  </head>
  <body>
    <p>Click on the square below:</p>
    <span id = "result"> </span>
                    <div id = "division" style = "background-color:blue;">
    This is Blue Square!!
    </div>
  </body>
</html>
```

This will produce following result –

# REMOVING DOM ELEMENTS

There may be a situation when you would like to remove one or more DOM elements from the document. JQuery provides two methods to handle the situation.

The empty( ) method remove all child nodes from the set of matched elements where as the method remove( expr ) method removes all matched elements from the DOM.

Here is the syntax for the method –

*selector*.remove( [ expr ])

or

*selector*.empty( )

You can pass optional parameter *expr* to filter the set of elements to be removed.

## Example

Following is an example where elements are being removed as soon as they are clicked –

```
<html>
  <head>
    <title>The jQuery Example</title>
    <script type = "text/javascript"
      src = "https://ajax.googleapis.com/ajax/libs/jquery/2.1.3/jquery.min.js">
    </script>

    <script type = "text/javascript" language = "javascript">
      $(document).ready(function() {
        $("div").click(function () {
          $(this).remove( );
        });
      });
    </script>
```

```
    <style>
      .div{ margin:10px;padding:12px; border:2px solid #666; width:60px;}
    </style>
  </head>

  <body>
    <p>Click on any square below:</p>
    <span id = "result"> </span>

    <div class = "div" style = "background-color:blue;"></div>
    <div class = "div" style = "background-color:green;"></div>
    <div class = "div" style = "background-color:red;"></div>
  </body>
</html>
```

This will produce following result –

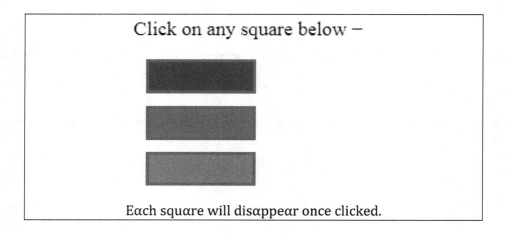

Click on any square below –

Each square will disappear once clicked.

# Inserting DOM Elements

There may be a situation when you would like to insert new one or more DOM elements in your existing document. JQuery provides various methods to insert elements at various locations.

The after( content ) method insert content after each of the matched elements where as the method before( content ) method inserts content before each of the matched elements.

Here is the syntax for the method –

*selector*.after( content )

or

*selector*.before( content )

Here content is what you want to insert. This could be HTML or simple text.

## Example

Following is an example where <div> elements are being inserted just before the clicked element –

```
<html>
 <head>
  <title>The jQuery Example</title>
  <script type = "text/javascript"
   src = "https://ajax.googleapis.com/ajax/libs/jquery/2.1.3/jquery.min.js">
  </script>

  <script type = "text/javascript" language = "javascript">
   $(document).ready(function() {
    $("div").click(function () {
     $(this).before('<div class="div"></div>' );
```

```
        });
      });
    </script>

    <style>
      .div{ margin:10px;padding:12px; border:2px solid #666; width:60px;}
    </style>
  </head>

  <body>
    <p>Click on any square below:</p>
    <span id = "result"> </span>

    <div class = "div" style = "background-color:blue;"></div>
    <div class = "div" style = "background-color:green;"></div>
    <div class = "div" style = "background-color:red;"></div>
  </body>
</html>
```

This will produce following result –

Click on any square below –

# DOM Manipulation Methods

Following table lists down all the methods which you can use to manipulate DOM elements –

| Sr.No. | Method & Description |
|--------|---------------------|
| 1 | **after( content )**<br><br>Insert content after each of the matched elements. |
| 2 | **append( content )**<br><br>Append content to the inside of every matched element. |
| 3 | **appendTo( selector )**<br><br>Append all of the matched elements to another, specified, set of elements. |
| 4 | **before( content )**<br><br>Insert content before each of the matched elements. |

| 5 | **clone( bool )** |
|---|---|
| | Clone matched DOM Elements, and all their event handlers, and select the clones. |
| 6 | **clone( )** |
| | Clone matched DOM Elements and select the clones. |
| 7 | **empty( )** |
| | Remove all child nodes from the set of matched elements. |
| 8 | **html( val )** |
| | Set the html contents of every matched element. |
| 9 | **html( )** |
| | Get the html contents (innerHTML) of the first matched element. |
| 10 | **insertAfter( selector )** |
| | Insert all of the matched elements after another, specified, set of elements. |

| 11 | **insertBefore( selector )** |
|---|---|
| | Insert all of the matched elements before another, specified, set of elements. |
| 12 | **prepend( content )** |
| | Prepend content to the inside of every matched element. |
| 13 | **prependTo( selector )** |
| | Prepend all of the matched elements to another, specified, set of elements. |
| 14 | **remove( expr )** |
| | Removes all matched elements from the DOM. |
| 15 | **replaceAll( selector )** |
| | Replaces the elements matched by the specified selector with the matched elements. |
| 16 | **replaceWith( content )** |
| | Replaces all matched elements with the specified HTML or DOM elements. |

| 17 | **text( val )** |
|----|----------------|
|    | Set the text contents of all matched elements. |
| 18 | **text( )** |
|    | Get the combined text contents of all matched elements. |
| 19 | **wrap( elem )** |
|    | Wrap each matched element with the specified element. |
| 20 | **wrap( html )** |
|    | Wrap each matched element with the specified HTML content. |
| 21 | **wrapAll( elem )** |
|    | Wrap all the elements in the matched set into a single wrapper element. |
| 22 | **wrapAll( html )** |
|    | Wrap all the elements in the matched set into a single wrapper element. |

| 23 | **wrapInner( elem )**<br><br>Wrap the inner child contents of each matched element (including text nodes) with a DOM element. |
|----|----|
| 24 | **wrapInner( html )**<br><br>Wrap the inner child contents of each matched element (including text nodes) with an HTML structure. |

# JQUERY - EVENTS HANDLING

We have the ability to create dynamic web pages by using events. Events are actions that can be detected by your Web Application.

Following are the examples events –

- A mouse click
- A web page loading
- Taking mouse over an element
- Submitting an HTML form
- A keystroke on your keyboard, etc.

When these events are triggered, you can then use a custom function to do pretty much whatever you want with the event. These custom functions call Event Handlers.

## BINDING EVENT HANDLERS

Using the jQuery Event Model, we can establish event handlers on DOM elements with the bind() method as follows –

```html
<html>
  <head>
    <title>The jQuery Example</title>
    <script type = "text/javascript"
      src = "https://ajax.googleapis.com/ajax/libs/jquery/2.1.3/jquery.min.js">
    </script>

    <script type = "text/javascript" language = "javascript">
      $(document).ready(function() {
        $('div').bind('click', function( event ){
          alert('Hi there!');
        });
      });
```

```
    </script>

    <style>
      .div{ margin:10px;padding:12px; border:2px solid #666; width:60px;}
    </style>
  </head>

  <body>
    <p>Click on any square below to see the result:</p>

    <div class = "div" style = "background-color:blue;">ONE</div>
    <div class = "div" style = "background-color:green;">TWO</div>
    <div class = "div" style = "background-color:red;">THREE</div>
  </body>
</html>
```

This code will cause the division element to respond to the click event; when a user clicks inside this division thereafter, the alert will be shown.

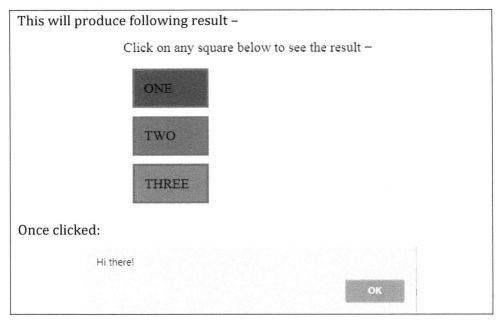

This will produce following result –

Click on any square below to see the result –

ONE

TWO

THREE

Once clicked:

Hi there!

OK

The full syntax of the bind() command is as follows –

*selector*.bind( eventType[, eventData], handler)

Following is the description of the parameters –

- eventType – A string containing a JavaScript event type, such as click or submit. Refer to the next section for a complete list of event types.
- eventData – This is optional parameter is a map of data that will be passed to the event handler.
- handler – A function to execute each time the event is triggered.\

## REMOVING EVENT HANDLERS

Typically, once an event handler is established, it remains in effect for the remainder of the life of the page. There may be a need when you would like to remove event handler.

jQuery provides the unbind() command to remove an exiting event handler. The syntax of unbind() is as follows –

*selector*.unbind(eventType, handler)

or

*selector*.unbind(eventType)

Following is the description of the parameters –

- eventType – A string containing a JavaScript event type, such as click or submit. Refer to the next section for a complete list of event types.
- handler – If provided, identifies the specific listener that's to be removed.

## EVENT TYPES

The following are cross platform and recommended event types which you can bind using JQuery –

## THE EVENT OBJECT

The callback function takes a single parameter; when the handler is called the JavaScript event object will be passed through it.

The event object is often unnecessary and the parameter is omitted, as sufficient context is usually available when the handler is bound to know exactly what needs to be done when the handler is triggered, however there are certain attributes which you would need to be accessed.

# THE EVENT ATTRIBUTES

The following event properties/attributes are available and safe to access in a platform independent manner –

```html
<html>
  <head>
    <title>The jQuery Example</title>
    <script type = "text/javascript"
     src = "https://ajax.googleapis.com/ajax/libs/jquery/2.1.3/jquery.min.js">
    </script>
    <script type = "text/javascript" language = "javascript">
      $(document).ready(function() {
        $('div').bind('click', function( event ){
          alert('Event type is ' + event.type);
          alert('pageX : ' + event.pageX);
          alert('pageY : ' + event.pageY);
          alert('Target : ' + event.target.innerHTML);
        });
      });
    </script>
    <style>
      .div{ margin:10px;padding:12px; border:2px solid #666; width:60px;}
    </style>
  </head>
  <body>
    <p>Click on any square below to see the result:</p>

    <div class = "div" style = "background-color:blue;">ONE</div>
    <div class = "div" style = "background-color:green;">TWO</div>
    <div class = "div" style = "background-color:red;">THREE</div>
  </body>
</html>
```

This will produce following result –

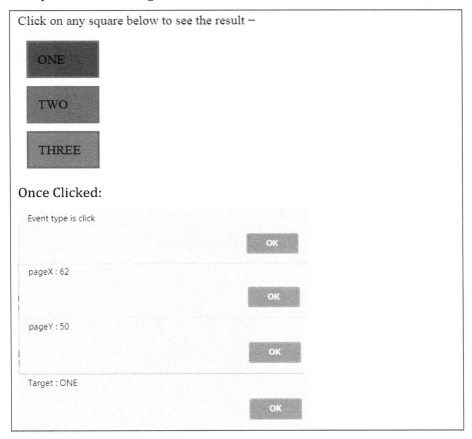

# THE EVENT METHODS

There is a list of methods which can be called on an Event Object –

| Sr.No. | Method & Description |
|--------|---------------------|
| 1 | **preventDefault()**<br><br>Prevents the browser from executing the default action. |
| 2 | **isDefaultPrevented()**<br><br>Returns whether event.preventDefault() was ever called on this event object. |
| 3 | **stopPropagation()**<br><br>Stops the bubbling of an event to parent elements, preventing any parent handlers from being notified of the event. |
| 4 | **isPropagationStopped()**<br><br>Returns whether event.stopPropagation() was ever called on this event object. |
| 5 | **stopImmediatePropagation()**<br><br>Stops the rest of the handlers from being executed. |

| 6 | isImmediatePropagationStopped() |
|---|---|
| | Returns whether event.stopImmediatePropagation() was ever called on this event object. |

# EVENT MANIPULATION METHODS

Following table lists down important event-related methods –

| Sr.No. | Method & Description |
|--------|----------------------|
| 1 | **bind( type, [data], fn )** <br><br> Binds a handler to one or more events (like click) for each matched element. Can also bind custom events. |
| 2 | **off( events [, selector ] [, handler(eventObject) ] )** <br><br> This does the opposite of live, it removes a bound live event. |
| 3 | **hover( over, out )** <br><br> Simulates hovering for example moving the mouse on, and off, an object. |

| 4 | **<u>on( events [, selector ] [, data ], handler )</u>** |
|---|---|
| | Binds a handler to an event (like click) for all current – and future – matched element. Can also bind custom events. |
| 5 | **<u>one( type, [data], fn )</u>** |
| | Binds a handler to one or more events to be executed once for each matched element. |
| 6 | **<u>ready( fn )</u>** |
| | Binds a function to be executed whenever the DOM is ready to be traversed and manipulated. |
| 7 | **<u>trigger( event, [data] )</u>** |
| | Trigger an event on every matched element. |
| 8 | **<u>triggerHandler( event, [data] )</u>** |
| | Triggers all bound event handlers on an element. |
| 9 | **<u>unbind( [type], [fn] )</u>** |
| | This does the opposite of bind, it removes bound events from each of the matched elements. |

# EVENT HELPER METHODS

jQuery also provides a set of event helper functions which can be used either to trigger an event to bind any event types mentioned above.

# TRIGGER METHODS

Following is an example which would triggers the blur event on all paragraphs –

$("p").blur();

# BINDING METHODS

Following is an example which would bind a click event on all the <div> –

```
$("div").click( function () {
   // do something here
});
```

Here is a complete list of all the support methods provided by jQuery –

| Sr.No. | Method & Description |
|--------|----------------------|
| 1 | **blur( )** <br><br> Triggers the blur event of each matched element. |
| 2 | **blur( fn )** <br><br> Bind a function to the blur event of each matched element. |

| 3 | **change( )** |
|---|---|
| | Triggers the change event of each matched element. |
| 4 | **change( fn )** |
| | Binds a function to the change event of each matched element. |
| 5 | **click( )** |
| | Triggers the click event of each matched element. |
| 6 | **click( fn )** |
| | Binds a function to the click event of each matched element. |
| 7 | **dblclick( )** |
| | Triggers the dblclick event of each matched element. |
| 8 | **dblclick( fn )** |
| | Binds a function to the dblclick event of each matched element. |
| 9 | **error( )** |
| | Triggers the error event of each matched element. |

| 10 | **error( fn )** |
|---|---|
| | Binds a function to the error event of each matched element. |
| 11 | **focus( )** |
| | Triggers the focus event of each matched element. |
| 12 | **focus( fn )** |
| | Binds a function to the focus event of each matched element. |
| 13 | **keydown( )** |
| | Triggers the keydown event of each matched element. |
| 14 | **keydown( fn )** |
| | Bind a function to the keydown event of each matched element. |
| 15 | **keypress( )** |
| | Triggers the keypress event of each matched element. |
| 16 | **keypress( fn )** |
| | Binds a function to the keypress event of each |

| | |
|---|---|
| | matched element. |
| 17 | **keyup( )**<br><br>Triggers the keyup event of each matched element. |
| 18 | **keyup( fn )**<br><br>Bind a function to the keyup event of each matched element. |
| 19 | **load( fn )**<br><br>Binds a function to the load event of each matched element. |
| 20 | **mousedown( fn )**<br><br>Binds a function to the mousedown event of each matched element. |
| 21 | **mouseenter( fn )**<br><br>Bind a function to the mouseenter event of each matched element. |
| 22 | **mouseleave( fn )**<br><br>Bind a function to the mouseleave event of each |

| | |
|---|---|
| | matched element. |
| 23 | **mousemove( fn )**<br><br>Bind a function to the mousemove event of each matched element. |
| 24 | **mouseout( fn )**<br><br>Bind a function to the mouseout event of each matched element. |
| 25 | **mouseover( fn )**<br><br>Bind a function to the mouseover event of each matched element. |
| 26 | **mouseup( fn )**<br><br>Bind a function to the mouseup event of each matched element. |
| 27 | **resize( fn )**<br><br>Bind a function to the resize event of each matched element. |
| 28 | **scroll( fn )**<br><br>Bind a function to the scroll event of each matched |

| | |
|---|---|
| | element. |
| 29 | **select( )**<br><br>Trigger the select event of each matched element. |
| 30 | **select( fn )**<br><br>Bind a function to the select event of each matched element. |
| 31 | **submit( )**<br><br>Trigger the submit event of each matched element. |
| 32 | **submit( fn )**<br><br>Bind a function to the submit event of each matched element. |
| 33 | **unload( fn )**<br><br>Binds a function to the unload event of each matched element. |

# JQuery - Ajax

AJAX is an acronym standing for Asynchronous JavaScript and XML and this technology helps us to load data from the server without a browser page refresh.

If you are new with AJAX, I would recommend you go through the Ajax Tutorial before proceeding further.

JQuery is a great tool which provides a rich set of AJAX methods to develop next generation web application.

## LOADING SIMPLE DATA

This is very easy to load any static or dynamic data using JQuery AJAX. JQuery provides load() method to do the job –

# Syntax

Here is the simple syntax for load() method –

```
[selector].load( URL, [data], [callback] );
```

Here is the description of all the parameters –

- URL – The URL of the server-side resource to which the request is sent. It could be a CGI, ASP, JSP, or PHP script which generates data dynamically or out of a database.
- data – This optional parameter represents an object whose properties are serialized into properly encoded parameters to be passed to the request. If specified, the request is made using the POST method. If omitted, the GET method is used.
- callback – A callback function invoked after the response data has been loaded into the elements of the matched set. The first parameter passed to this function is the response text received from the server and second parameter is the status code.

**Example**

Consider the following HTML file with a small JQuery coding –

```html
<html>
  <had>
    <title>The jQuery Example</title>
    <script type = "text/javascript"
      src = "https://ajax.googleapis.com/ajax/libs/jquery/2.1.3/jquery.min.js">
    </script>

    <script type = "text/javascript" language = "javascript">
      $(document).ready(function() {
        $("#driver").click(function(event){
          $('#stage').load('/jquery/result.html');
        });
      });
    </script>
  </head>

  <body>
    <p>Click on the button to load /jquery/result.html file –</p>

    <div id = "stage" style = "background-color:cc0;">
      STAGE
    </div>

    <input type = "button" id = "driver" value = "Load Data" />
  </body>
</html>
```

Here **load()** initiates an Ajax request to the specified URL /jquery/result.html file. After loading this file, all the content would be populated inside <div> tagged with ID *stage*. Assuming, our /jquery/result.html file has just one HTML line –

```html
<h1>THIS IS RESULT...</h1>
```

When you click the given button, then result.html file gets loaded.

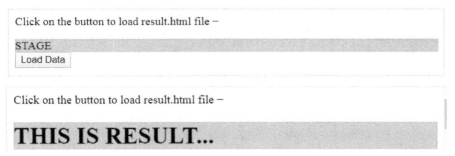

# GETTING JSON DATA

There would be a situation when server would return JSON string against your request. JQuery utility function getJSON() parses the returned JSON string and makes the resulting string available to the callback function as first parameter to take further action.

## Syntax

Here is the simple syntax for getJSON() method –

```
[selector].getJSON( URL, [data], [callback] );
```

Here is the description of all the parameters –

- URL – The URL of the server-side resource contacted via the GET method.
- data – An object whose properties serve as the name/value pairs used to construct a query string to be appended to the URL, or a preformatted and encoded query string.
- callback – A function invoked when the request completes. The data value resulting from digesting the response body as a JSON string is passed as the first parameter to this callback, and the status as the second.

**Example**

Consider the following HTML file with a small JQuery coding –

```html
<html>
 <head>
  <title>The jQuery Example</title>
  <script type = "text/javascript"
   src = "https://ajax.googleapis.com/ajax/libs/jquery/2.1.3/jquery.min.js">
  </script>

  <script type = "text/javascript" language = "javascript">
   $(document).ready(function() {
    $("#driver").click(function(event){

     $.getJSON('/jquery/result.json', function(jd) {
      $('#stage').html('<p> Name: ' + jd.name + '</p>');
      $('#stage').append('<p>Age : ' + jd.age+ '</p>');
      $('#stage').append('<p> Sex: ' + jd.sex+ '</p>');
     });

    });
   });
  </script>
 </head>

 <body>
  <p>Click on the button to load result.json file –</p>

  <div id = "stage" style = "background-color:#eee;">
   STAGE
  </div>

  <input type = "button" id = "driver" value = "Load Data" />
 </body>
</html>
```

Here JQuery utility method getJSON() initiates an Ajax request to the specified URL result.json file. After loading this file, all the content would be passed to the callback function which finally would be populated inside <div> tagged with ID *stage*. Assuming, our result.json file has following json formatted content −

```
{
  "name": "Zara Ali",
  "age" : "67",
  "sex": "female"
}
```

When you click the given button, then result.json file gets loaded.

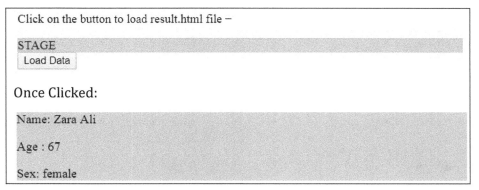

# PASSING DATA TO THE SERVER

Many times you collect input from the user and you pass that input to the server for further processing. JQuery AJAX made it easy enough to pass collected data to the server using data parameter of any available Ajax method.

## Example

This example demonstrate how can pass user input to a web server script which would send the same result back and we would print it −

```html
<html>
  <head>
    <title>The jQuery Example</title>
    <script type = "text/javascript"
      src = "https://ajax.googleapis.com/ajax/libs/jquery/2.1.3/jquery.min.js">
    </script>

    <script type = "text/javascript" language = "javascript">
      $(document).ready(function() {
        $("#driver").click(function(event){
          var name = $("#name").val();
          $("#stage").load('/jquery/result.php', {"name":name} );
        });
      });
    </script>
  </head>

  <body>
    <p>Enter your name and click on the button:</p>
    <input type = "input" id = "name" size = "40" /><br />

    <div id = "stage" style = "background-color:cc0;">
      STAGE
    </div>

    <input type = "button" id = "driver" value = "Show Result" />
  </body>
</html>
```

Here is the code written in result.php script −

```php
<?php
  if( $_REQUEST["name"] ){
    $name = $_REQUEST['name'];
    echo "Welcome ". $name;
  }
?>
```

Now you can enter any text in the given input box and then click "Show Result" button to see what you have entered in the input box.

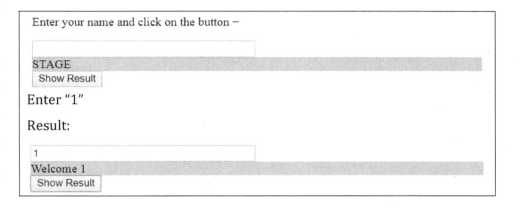

Enter your name and click on the button −

STAGE
Show Result

Enter "1"

Result:

1

Welcome 1
Show Result

# JQuery AJAX Methods

You have seen basic concept of AJAX using JQuery. Following table lists down all important JQuery AJAX methods which you can use based your programming need −

| Sr.No. | Methods & Description |
|---|---|
| 1 | **jQuery.ajax( options )**<br><br>Load a remote page using an HTTP request. |
| 2 | **jQuery.ajaxSetup( options )**<br><br>Setup global settings for AJAX requests. |

| | |
|---|---|
| 3 | **jQuery.get( url, [data], [callback], [type] )**<br><br>Load a remote page using an HTTP GET request. |
| 4 | **jQuery.getJSON( url, [data], [callback] )**<br><br>Load JSON data using an HTTP GET request. |
| 5 | **jQuery.getScript( url, [callback] )**<br><br>Loads and executes a JavaScript file using an HTTP GET request. |
| 6 | **jQuery.post( url, [data], [callback], [type] )**<br><br>Load a remote page using an HTTP POST request. |
| 7 | **load( url, [data], [callback] )**<br><br>Load HTML from a remote file and inject it into the DOM. |
| 8 | **serialize( )**<br><br>Serializes a set of input elements into a string of data. |

| 9 | **serializeArray( )** |
|---|---|
| | Serializes all forms and form elements like the .serialize() method but returns a JSON data structure for you to work with. |

# JQUERY AJAX EVENTS

You can call various JQuery methods during the life cycle of AJAX call progress. Based on different events/stages following methods are available –

| Sr.No. | Methods & Description |
|--------|----------------------|
| 1 | **ajaxComplete( callback )**<br><br>Attach a function to be executed whenever an AJAX request completes. |
| 2 | **ajaxStart( callback )**<br><br>Attach a function to be executed whenever an AJAX request begins and there is none already active. |
| 3 | **ajaxError( callback )**<br><br>Attach a function to be executed whenever an AJAX request fails. |
| 4 | **ajaxSend( callback )**<br><br>Attach a function to be executed before an AJAX request is sent. |

| 5 | **ajaxStop( callback )**

Attach a function to be executed whenever all AJAX requests have ended. |
| 6 | **ajaxSuccess( callback )**

Attach a function to be executed whenever an AJAX request completes successfully. |

# JQUERY - EFFECTS

jQuery provides a trivially simple interface for doing various kind of amazing effects. jQuery methods allow us to quickly apply commonly used effects with a minimum configuration. This tutorial covers all the important jQuery methods to create visual effects.

## SHOWING AND HIDING ELEMENTS

The commands for showing and hiding elements are pretty much what we would expect – show() to show the elements in a wrapped set and hide() to hide them.

### Syntax

Here is the simple syntax for show() method –

```
[selector].show( speed, [callback] );
```

Here is the description of all the parameters –

- speed – A string representing one of the three predefined speeds ("slow", "normal", or "fast") or the number of milliseconds to run the animation (e.g. 1000).
- callback – This optional parameter represents a function to be executed whenever the animation completes; executes once for each element animated against.

Following is the simple syntax for hide() method –

```
[selector].hide( speed, [callback] );
```

Here is the description of all the parameters –

- speed – A string representing one of the three predefined speeds ("slow", "normal", or "fast") or the number of milliseconds to run the animation (e.g. 1000).

- callback – This optional parameter represents a function to be executed whenever the animation completes; executes once for each element animated against.

## Example

Consider the following HTML file with a small JQuery coding –

```html
<html>
  <head>
    <title>The jQuery Example</title>
    <script type = "text/javascript"
      src = "https://ajax.googleapis.com/ajax/libs/jquery/2.1.3/jquery.min.js">
    </script>

    <script type = "text/javascript" language = "javascript">
      $(document).ready(function() {
        $("#show").click(function () {
          $(".mydiv").show( 1000 );
        });
        $("#hide").click(function () {
          $(".mydiv").hide( 1000 );
        });
      });
    </script>

    <style>
      .mydiv{
        margin:10px;
        padding:12px;
        border:2px solid #666;
        width:100px;
        height:100px;
      }
    </style>
  </head>

  <body>
    <div class = "mydiv">
      This is a SQUARE
    </div>

    <input id = "hide" type = "button" value = "Hide" />
```

95

```
    <input id = "show" type = "button" value = "Show" />
  </body>
</html>
```

This will produce following result –

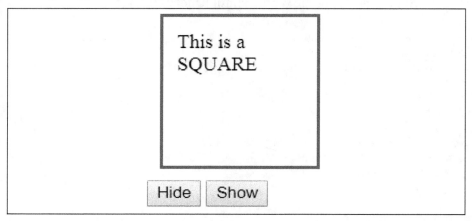

# TOGGLING THE ELEMENTS

jQuery provides methods to toggle the display state of elements between revealed or hidden. If the element is initially displayed, it will be hidden; if hidden, it will be shown.

## Syntax

Here is the simple syntax for one of the toggle() methods –

```
[selector]..toggle([speed][, callback]);
```

Here is the description of all the parameters –

- speed – A string representing one of the three predefined speeds ("slow", "normal", or "fast") or the number of milliseconds to run the animation (e.g. 1000).
- callback – This optional parameter represents a function to be executed whenever the animation completes; executes once for each element animated against.

## Example

We can animate any element, such as a simple <div> containing an image –

```html
<html>
  <head>
    <title>The jQuery Example</title>
    <script type = "text/javascript"
      src = "https://ajax.googleapis.com/ajax/libs/jquery/2.1.3/jquery.min.js">
    </script>

    <script type = "text/javascript" language = "javascript">
      $(document).ready(function() {
        $(".clickme").click(function(event){
          $(".target").toggle('slow', function(){
            $(".log").text('Transition Complete');
          });
        });
      });
    </script>
```

```
  <style>
    .clickme{
      margin:10px;
      padding:12px;
      border:2px solid #666;
      width:100px;
      height:50px;
    }
  </style>
</head>
<body>
  <div class = "content">
    <div class = "clickme">Click Me</div>
    <div class = "target">
      <img src = "./images/jquery.jpg" alt = "jQuery" />
    </div>
    <div class = "log"></div>
  </div>
</body>
</html>
```

This will produce following result –

# JQuery Effect Methods

You have seen basic concept of jQuery Effects. Following table lists down all the important methods to create different kind of effects –

| Sr.No. | Methods & Description |
|--------|----------------------|
| 1 | **animate( params, [duration, easing, callback] )**<br><br>A function for making custom animations. |
| 2 | **fadeIn( speed, [callback] )**<br><br>Fade in all matched elements by adjusting their opacity and firing an optional callback after completion. |
| 3 | **fadeOut( speed, [callback] )**<br><br>Fade out all matched elements by adjusting their opacity to 0, then setting display to "none" and firing an optional callback after completion. |
| 4 | **fadeTo( speed, opacity, callback )**<br><br>Fade the opacity of all matched elements to a specified opacity and firing an optional callback after completion. |

| 5 | **hide( )** |
|---|---|
| | Hides each of the set of matched elements if they are shown. |
| 6 | **hide( speed, [callback] )** |
| | Hide all matched elements using a graceful animation and firing an optional callback after completion. |
| 7 | **show( )** |
| | Displays each of the set of matched elements if they are hidden. |
| 8 | **show( speed, [callback] )** |
| | Show all matched elements using a graceful animation and firing an optional callback after completion. |
| 9 | **slideDown( speed, [callback] )** |
| | Reveal all matched elements by adjusting their height and firing an optional callback after completion. |
| 10 | **slideToggle( speed, [callback] )** |
| | Toggle the visibility of all matched elements by adjusting their height and firing an optional callback after completion. |

| 11 | **slideUp( speed, [callback] )** |
|---|---|
| | Hide all matched elements by adjusting their height and firing an optional callback after completion. |
| 12 | **stop( [clearQueue, gotoEnd ])** |
| | Stops all the currently running animations on all the specified elements. |
| 13 | **toggle( )** |
| | Toggle displaying each of the set of matched elements. |
| 14 | **toggle( speed, [callback] )** |
| | Toggle displaying each of the set of matched elements using a graceful animation and firing an optional callback after completion. |
| 15 | **toggle( switch )** |
| | Toggle displaying each of the set of matched elements based upon the switch (true shows all elements, false hides all elements). |

| 16 | jQuery.fx.off |
|---|---|
| | Globally disable all animations. |

# UI LIBRARY BASED EFFECTS

To use these effects you can either download latest jQuery UI Library jquery-ui-1.11.4.custom.zip from jQuery UI Library or use Google CDN to use it in the similar way as we have done for jQuery.

We have used Google CDN for jQuery UI using following code snippet in the HTML page so we can use jQuery UI –

```
<head>
  <script src = "https://ajax.googleapis.com/ajax/libs/jqueryui/1.11.3/jquery-ui.min.js">
  </script>
</head>
```

| Sr.No. | Methods & Description |
|---|---|
| 1 | **Blind** |
| | Blinds the element away or shows it by blinding it in. |
| 2 | **Bounce** |
| | Bounces the element vertically or horizontally n-times. |

| 3 | **Clip** |
| | Clips the element on or off, vertically or horizontally. |

| 4 | **Drop** |
| | Drops the element away or shows it by dropping it in. |

| 5 | **Explode** |
| | Explodes the element into multiple pieces. |

| 6 | **Fold** |
| | Folds the element like a piece of paper. |

| 7 | **Highlight** |
| | Highlights the background with a defined color. |

| 8 | **Puff** |
| | Scale and fade out animations create the puff effect. |

| 9 | **Pulsate** |
| | Pulsates the opacity of the element multiple times. |

| 10 | **Scale** |
| | Shrink or grow an element by a percentage factor. |

| 11 | **Shake** |
| | Shakes the element vertically or horizontally n-times. |

| 12 | **Size** |
| | Resize an element to a specified width and height. |

| 13 | **Slide** |
| | Slides the element out of the viewport. |

| 14 | **Transfer** |
| | Transfers the outline of an element to another. |

# JQUERY - INTERACTIONS

Interactions could be added basic mouse-based behaviours to any element. Using with interactions, We can create sortable lists, resizeable elements, drag & drop behaviours.Interactions also make great building blocks for more complex widgets and applications.

| Sr.No. | Interactions & Description |
|--------|---------------------------|
| 1 | **Drag able**<br><br>Enable drag able functionality on any DOM element. |
| 2 | **Drop able**<br><br>Enable any DOM element to be drop able. |
| 3 | **Resize able**<br><br>Enable any DOM element to be resize-able. |
| 4 | **Select able**<br><br>Enable a DOM element (or group of elements) to be selectable. |

| 5 | **<u>Sort αble</u>** |
|---|---|
|   | Enαble α group of DOM elements to be sortαble. |

# JQUERY - WIDGETS

A jQuery UI widget is a specialized jQuery plug-in.Using plug-in, we can apply behaviours to the elements. However, plug-ins lack some built-in capabilities, such as a way to associate data with its elements, expose methods, merge options with defaults, and control the plug-in's lifetime.

| Sr.No. | Widgets & Description |
|--------|----------------------|
| 1 | **Accordion**<br><br>Enable to collapse the content, that is broken into logical sections. |
| 2 | **Autocomplete**<br><br>Enable to provides the suggestions while you type into the field. |
| 3 | **Button**<br><br>Button is an input of type submit and an anchor. |
| 4 | **Datepicker**<br><br>It is to open an interactive calendar in a small overlay. |

| 5 | **<u>Dialog</u>** |
|---|---|
| | Dialog boxes are one of the nice ways of presenting information on an HTML page. |
| 6 | **<u>Menu</u>** |
| | Menu shows list of items. |
| 7 | **<u>Progressbar</u>** |
| | It shows the progress information. |
| 8 | **<u>Select menu</u>** |
| | Enable a style able select element/elements. |
| 9 | **<u>Slider</u>** |
| | The basic slider is horizontal and has a single handle that can be moved with the mouse or by using the arrow keys. |
| 10 | **<u>Spinner</u>** |
| | It provides a quick way to select one value from a set. |

| 11 | **Tabs** |
| --- | --- |
| | It is used to swap between content that is broken into logical sections. |
| 12 | **Tooltip** |
| | Its provides the tips for the users. |

# JQUERY - THEMING

Jquery has two different styling themes as A And B.Each with different colors for buttons, bars, content blocks, and so on.

The syntax of J query theming as shown below –

```
<div data-role = "page" data-theme = "a|b">
```

A Simple of A theming Example as shown below –

```
<!DOCTYPE html>
<html>
  <head>
    <meta name = "viewport" content = "width = device-width, initial-scale = 1">
    <link rel = "stylesheet"
      href = "https://code.jquery.com/mobile/1.4.5/jquery.mobile-1.4.5.min.css">

    <script src = "https://code.jquery.com/jquery-1.11.3.min.js">
    </script>
    <script src = "https://code.jquery.com/jquery-1.11.3.min.js">
    </script>
    <script
      src = "https://code.jquery.com/mobile/1.4.5/jquery.mobile-1.4.5.min.js">
    </script>
  </head>

  <body>
    <div data-role = "page" id = "pageone" data-theme = "a" >
     <div data-role = "header">
       <h1>My Wed</h1>
     </div>
     <div data-role = "main" class = "ui-content">
       <p>Text link</p>
       <a href = "#">A Standard Text Link</a>
       <a href = "#" class = "ui-btn">Link Button</a>
```

```
<p>A List View:</p>

<ul data-role = "listview" data-autodividers = "true" data-inset = "true">
  <li><a href = "#">Android </a></li>
  <li><a href = "#">IOS</a></li>
</ul>

<label for = "fullname">Input Field:</label>
<input type = "text" name = "fullname" id = "fullname"
  placeholder = "Name..">
<label for = "switch">Toggle Switch:</label>

<select name = "switch" id = "switch" data-role = "slider">
  <option value = "on">On</option>
  <option value = "off" selected>Off</option>
</select>

</div>
<div data-role = "footer">
  <h1>My Wed</h1>
</div>
</div>
</body>
</html>
```

This should produce following result –

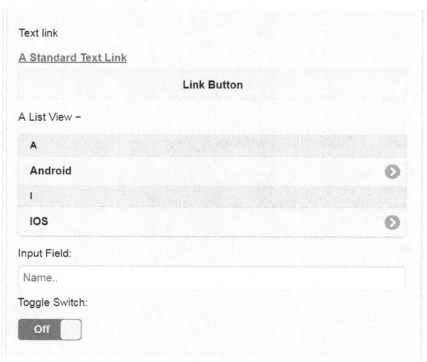

A Simple of B theming Example as shown below –

```
<!DOCTYPE html>
<html>
  <head>
    <meta name = "viewport" content = "width = device-width, initial-scale = 1">
    <link rel = "stylesheet"
      href = "https://code.jquery.com/mobile/1.4.5/jquery.mobile-1.4.5.min.css">
    <script src = "https://code.jquery.com/jquery-1.11.3.min.js">
    </script>
    <script src = "https://code.jquery.com/jquery-1.11.3.min.js">
    </script>
    <script
      src = "https://code.jquery.com/mobile/1.4.5/jquery.mobile-1.4.5.min.js">
    </script>
```

```html
</head>

<body>
  <div data-role = "page" id = "pageone" data-theme = "b">
    <div data-role = "header">
      <h1>My Wed</h1>
    </div>

    <div data-role = "main" class = "ui-content">
      <p>Text link</p>
      <a href = "#">A Standard Text Link</a>
      <a href = "#" class = "ui-btn">Link Button</a>
      <p>A List View:</p>

      <ul data-role = "listview" data-autodividers = "true" data-inset = "true">
        <li><a href = "#">Android </a></li>
        <li><a href = "#">IOS</a></li>
      </ul>

      <label for = "fullname">Input Field:</label>
      <input type = "text" name = "fullname" id = "fullname"
        placeholder = "Name..">
      <label for = "switch">Toggle Switch:</label>

      <select name = "switch" id = "switch" data-role = "slider">
        <option value = "on">On</option>
        <option value = "off" selected>Off</option>
      </select>

    </div>
    <div data-role = "footer">
      <h1>My Wed</h1>
    </div>
  </div>
 </body>
</html>
```

This should produce following result –

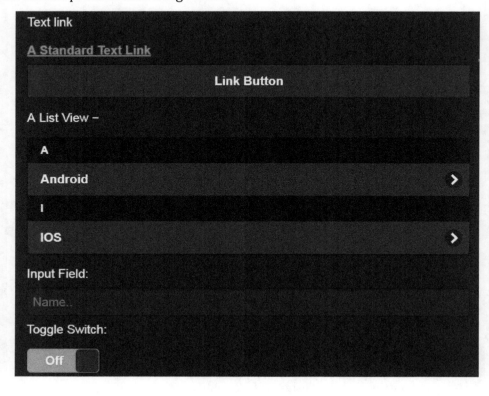

# JQuery - Utilities

Jquery provides serveral utilities in the formate of $(name space). These methods are helpful to complete the programming tasks.a few of the utility methods are as show below.

# $.trim()

$.trim() is used to Removes leading and trailing whitespace

$.trim( "   lots of extra whitespace   " );

# $.each()

$.each() is used to Iterates over arrays and objects

```
$.each([ "foo", "bar", "baz" ], function( idx, val ) {
  console.log( "element " + idx + " is " + val );
});

$.each({ foo: "bar", baz: "bim" }, function( k, v ) {
  console.log( k + " : " + v );
});
```

.each() can be called on a selection to iterate over the elements contained in the selection. .each(), not $.each(), should be used for iterating over elements in a selection.

# $.inArray()

$.inArray() is used to Returns a value's index in an array, or -1 if the value is not in the array.

```
var myArray = [ 1, 2, 3, 5 ];
if ( $.inArray( 4, myArray ) !== -1 ) {
  console.log( "found it!" );
}
```

# $.extend()

$.extend() is used to Changes the properties of the first object using the properties of subsequent objects.

```
var firstObject = { foo: "bar", a: "b" };
var secondObject = { foo: "baz" };

var newObject = $.extend( firstObject, secondObject );

console.log( firstObject.foo );
console.log( newObject.foo );
```

# $.proxy()

$.proxy() is used to Returns a function that will always run in the provided scope — that is, sets the meaning of this inside the passed function to the second argument

```
var myFunction = function() {
  console.log( this );
};

var myObject = {
  foo: "bar"
};

myFunction(); // window

var myProxyFunction = $.proxy( myFunction, myObject );

myProxyFunction();d
```

# $.browser

$.browser is used to give the information about browsers

```
jQuery.each( jQuery.browser, function( i, val ) {
  $( "<div>" + i + " : <span>" + val + "</span>" )
  .appendTo( document.body );
});
```

# $.contains()

$.contains() is used to returns true if the DOM element provided by the second argument is a descendant of the DOM element provided by the first argument, whether it is a direct child or nested more deeply.

```
$.contains( document.documentElement, document.body );
$.contains( document.body, document.documentElement );
```

# $.data()

$.data() is used to give the information about data

```
<html lang = "en">
 <head>
   <title>jQuery.data demo</title>
   <script src = "https://code.jquery.com/jquery-1.10.2.js">
   </script>
 </head>

 <body>
  <div>
    The values stored were <span></span>
     and <span></span>
  </div>

  <script>
   var div = $( "div" )[ 0 ];

   jQuery.data( div, "test", {
     first: 25,
     last: "tutorials"
   });
```

117

```
    $( "span:first" ).text( jQuery.data( div, "test" ).first );
    $( "span:last" ).text( jQuery.data( div, "test" ).last );
  </script>
 </body>
</html>
```

output would be as follows

The values stored were 25 and tutorials

# $.fn.extend()

$.fn.extend() is used to extends the jQuery prototype

```
<html lang = "en">
 <head>
  <script src = "https://code.jquery.com/jquery-1.10.2.js">
  </script>
 </head>

<body>
  <label><input type = "checkbox" name = "android">
   Android</label>
  <label><input type = "checkbox" name = "ios"> IOS</label>
  <script>
   jQuery.fn.extend({
    check: function() {
     return this.each(function() {
      this.checked = true;
     });
    },
    uncheck: function() {
     return this.each(function() {
      this.checked = false;
     });
    }
   });
   // Use the newly created .check() method
   $( "input[type = 'checkbox']" ).check();
```

```
    </script>
  </body>
</html>
```

It provides the output as shown below –

☑ Android ☑ ios

# $.isWindow()

$.isWindow() is used to recognise the window

```
<!doctype html>
<html lang = "en">
  <head>
    <meta charset = "utf-8">
    <title>jQuery.isWindow demo</title>
    <script src = "https://code.jquery.com/jquery-1.10.2.js">
    </script>
  </head>

  <body>
    Is 'window' a window? <b></b>

    <script>
      $( "b" ).append( "" + $.isWindow( window ) );
    </script>
  </body>
</html>
```
It provides the output as shown below –

# $.now()

It returns a number which is representing the current time

```
(new Date).getTime()
```

# $.isXMLDoc()

$.isXMLDoc() checks whether a file is an xml or not

```
jQuery.isXMLDoc( document )
 jQuery.isXMLDoc( document.body )
```

# $.globalEval()

$.globalEval() is used to execute the javascript globally

```
function test() {
  jQuery.globalEval( "var newVar = true;" )
}
test();
```

# $.dequeue()

$.dequeue() is used to execute the next function in the queue

```html
<!doctype html>
<html lang = "en">
  <head>
    <meta charset = "utf-8">
    <title>jQuery.dequeue demo</title>

    <style>
      div {
        margin: 3px;
        width: 50px;
        position: absolute;
        height: 50px;
        left: 10px;
        top: 30px;
        background-color: green;
        border-radius: 50px;
      }
      div.red {
        background-color: blue;
      }
    </style>
```

```
<script src = "https://code.jquery.com/jquery-1.10.2.js"></script>
</head>

<body>
  <button>Start</button>
  <div></div>

  <script>
    $( "button" ).click(function() {
      $( "div" )
      .animate({ left: '+ = 400px' }, 2000 )
      .animate({ top: '0px' }, 600 )

      .queue(function() {
        $( this ).toggleClass( "red" );
        $.dequeue( this );
      })

      .animate({ left:'10px', top:'30px' }, 700 );
    });
  </script>
</body>
</html>
```
It provides the output as shown below –

121

www.ingramcontent.com/pod-product-compliance
Lightning Source LLC
LaVergne TN
LVHW052302060326
832902LV00021B/3673